COLORFUL PORTLAND LOCATIONS

Please note all the information was correct at the time of publication, but as with all things in life it is subject to change. Happy exploring!

1. Planning to be in Portland the 2nd Sunday in August? Ditch the car and pedal your way across many of Portland's iconic bridges during **Providence Bridge Pedal**. Experience Portland in a whole new way as you ride under the 400-foot cathedral-like arches on the St. Johns Bridge. There is something for everyone with multiple distance options for families and die-hard bikers. providencebridgepedal.org

2. Just 10 miles from Portland, a trip to **Sauvie Island** is a wonderful escape from the city. Whether you're picking out that perfect pumpkin, searching for seasonal berries or enjoying a farm dinner, exploring this island is sure to please all your senses! sauvieisland.org

3. Ready for a BIG Portland welcome? The steel and concrete **Paul Bunyan Statue** stands 31 feet tall and towers over the north Portland Kenton neighborhood, where he has lived since 1959. In 2009, the mighty Paul Bunyan Statue was added to the National Register of Historic Places. historickenton.com

4. Portland's first public rose garden is located at **Peninsula Park** in North Portland. For maximum sensory impact, plan to visit in June, when the roses are in full bloom...and full aroma! The park, designed in the formal style of the early 1900s, also boasts Portland's first community center, a historically-designated bandstand and Portland's second oldest playground. portlandoregon.gov/parks

5. The smell of made-to-order mini doughnuts greets your nose when you walk into **Pip's Original Doughnuts**. These bite-sized gems come in spectacularly simple yet original flavors - raw honey and sea salt is our fav. Add a cup of their house made chai and you'll be all fueled up to explore Portland. instagram.com/pipsoriginal

6. The Beverly Cleary Sculpture Garden located on the west side of **Grant Park**, brings the familiar characters of Ramona Quimby, Henry Huggins and his dog, Ribsy, alive. Many of the stories by this famous local author are based in the neighborhood surrounding the park. Look for the street map outside the sculpture area for a literary neighborhood adventure! portlandoregon.gov/parks

7. "Drop in" to the **Burnside Skatepark**, located underneath the Burnside Bridge on the east side of the Willamette River, to see or skate with some of Portland's most colorful carvers. Built without permission by the skateboard community, it is now a sanctioned public skate park. burnsideskatepark.blogspot.com

8. Want to experience Portland like the locals do? Then grab your bike, walking shoes, disco outfit or scooter and head to the nearest **Sunday Parkways** route. Held monthly May-September, this City of Portland event is presented by Kaiser Permanente to promote healthy, active living, as well as foster community and economic development in Portland's neighborhoods. portlandsundayparkways.org

9. It's probably best to park your car and explore **Ladd's Addition**, Portland's oldest residential neighborhood, on foot. It's easy to get lost in the hexagonal street design, which is at odds with the traditional street grid pattern surrounding the neighborhood. The tree-lined streets are an eclectic museum of early 20th century architecture. William S. Ladd designed and built the neighborhood in 1891 around a central traffic circle with four diamond-shaped rose gardens. This carefully preserved neighborhood is recognized on the National Register of Historic Places.

10. **MAX (Metropolitan Area Express) Light Rail** trains are the cornerstone of an enviable public transportation system in Portland. Want to maximize your time exploring the city? Hop on a color-coded train at one of 97 stations in & around Portland to get to your next destination quickly and efficiently. With east/west and north/south options and short waits (trains run 15 minutes or better!), ditch the car and enjoy the scenery on your way to your next Portland adventure. trimet.org

11. Near the Sellwood Bridge, the **Oaks Park Skating Rink** is the largest on the West Coast and the only rink in the country with an organist playing a live pipe organ. Look for the mammoth Wurlitzer Organ, that was originally in the old Broadway Theater, hanging over the center of the rink. Put on your skates and "shoot the duck" on the wavy floor on the east end of the rink. oakspark.com

12. Just 50 miles outside of Portland, **Mount Hood** is Oregon's highest peak and the fourth largest in the Cascade Mountain Range. She shines majestically over the Columbia River Gorge, an area seemingly designed by the gods of outdoor recreation. Mt. Hood's slopes beg to be climbed, skied, snowboarded and hiked. Explore the lakes and rivers of its foothills for summer adventures.

13. The fully accessible **Trillium Trail**, part of the Tryon Creek State Natural Area, is a paved 0.35-mile loop designed to accommodate wheelchairs and hikers of all abilities, complete with interpretive signs and drinking fountains along the way. Located minutes from downtown in southwest Portland, there are all kinds of opportunities to explore Oregon's only major state park within a metropolitan area. oregonstateparks.org

14. Soar 500 feet over the city in just 4 minutes! The **Portland Aerial Tram** connects Portland's South Waterfront District to the OSHU (Oregon Health & Science University) Campus. At the top, take in splendid city and mountain views or hike the trails on Marquam Hill that are part of the 4T trail system (see #18). gobytram.com

15. Leave your car behind to explore **Tilikum Crossing** ("Bridge of the People"), Portland's newest bridge in 40 years. This addition to Portland's city scape is the largest car-free bridge in the United States, open only to public transportation, bicycles and pedestrians. The cables were designed to reflect the silhouette of Mt. Hood, visible to the east from center span on a clear day. portlandoregon.gov/transportation

COLORFUL PORTLAND LOCATIONS

16 Over 200 exhibits provide interactive science and technology exploration at **OMSI (Oregon Museum of Science & Industry)**. One of the museum's star attractions is docked just outside the door on the Willamette River. The USS Blueback Submarine (SS-581) is the US Navy's last non-nuclear submarine. Well-used by the Navy for 31 years, one can only imagine the stories this ship could tell! omsi.edu

17 A visit to one of Portland's vibrant farmers markets should be high on your list of must-experience stops. **Portland Farmers Market** has been bringing the best of the country to urban Portland since 1992. With more than 200 vendors at multiple neighborhood markets (the Portland State University market is open year-round), you are sure to find something to satisfy every appetite. portlandfarmersmarket.org

18 The 4T - Trail, Tram, Trolley and Train – is one of the best ways to explore Portland. The first T (Trail), is a 4-mile hike on the Marquam Trail to Portland's highest point - **Council Crest Park**. The 180-degree view of Portland as well as views of five Cascade Mountains (Hood, St. Helens, Adams, Jefferson and Rainier) will be your reward for reaching the top. It's mostly downhill from here as you make your way to the subsequent Ts. portlandoregon.gov/parks

19 Opened in 1888 with the donation of a grizzly bear and a brown bear, the **Oregon Zoo** is one of the oldest zoos west of the Mississippi. Situated in beautiful Washington Park, it now is home to around 2,000 animals and 200 species, many of which are endangered in their natural habitats. See some of the world's most amazing animals and help create a better future for wildlife. In case you were wondering, our illustration is a colorful mandrill. oregonzoo.org

20 Racing through the winding residential streets of Washington Park on creatively customized kiddie bikes, adults test their wits at furiously fast speeds. The adventurous sport of **Zoobombing** is not for the faint of heart, nor children! Occurs year-round on Sunday nights.

21 During the spring and summer for more than 25 years, teams practicing in their **Dragon Boats** dot the Willamette River near the Hawthorne Bridge. The Portland Rose Festival "Awakening of the Dragons" ceremony kicks off dragon boat season with firecrackers, drumming and lion dancing. The season culminates in June with Portland Rose Festival Dragon Boat Race, when 60 different teams compete in the boats provided through the Portland-Kaohsiung Sister City Association. pksca.net

22 Feel like Bratwurst or Korean Tacos? Fried onions or reindeer sausage? Explore the diverse food scene in Portland at one of more than 500 **Food Carts** around town. You will find carts all over the city, with an entire city block full of savory bites downtown at SW Alder Street & 11th Avenue. foodcartsportland.com

23 Hankering for a bacon-topped maple bar at 2AM? You'll find it, and more than 50 other eclectic options, at **Voodoo Doughnut**. Founded in 2003, Voodoo has become a Portland institution. The original & most popular location is in Old Town. voodoodoughnut.com

24 Established in 1974, **Portland Saturday Market** showcases a variety of arts & crafts sold by local Pacific Northwest artisans. This Portland tradition can be found in the Old Town /Chinatown neighborhood on Saturdays and Sundays through Christmas Eve. portlandsaturdaymarket.com

25 Plan to get lost at **Powell's City of Books** - the largest independent bookstore in the world. Powell's encompasses an entire city block and houses more than one million new, used, rare and out-of-print books purposefully mingled together in 3,500 sections on three floors. A true bibliophile's paradise! powells.com

26 The **Portland Oregon Sign™**, also known as the "White Stag" sign, overlooks the river in Old Town. The sign was originally built in 1940 and is listed on the National Register of Historic Places. A Portland holiday tradition is the illumination of the stag's nose to red. portlandoregon.gov

27 Enter the tranquil **Lan Su Chinese Garden** and you quickly forget urban downtown Portland is just outside the gates. The garden, designed in 1999 in collaboration with Portland's sister city Suzhou, is modeled after the Ming Dynasty gardens of China and offers visitors an accurate glimpse of Chinese culture and history. lansugarden.org

28 The Pearl District, including **Tanner Springs Park**, is located on an old wetland fed by streams that flowed from the hills of nearby Southwest Portland en route to the Willamette River. The park is a series of connected springs and ponds with plenty of grass to relax or run. A tranquil oasis in the middle of one of Portland's fastest-growing neighborhoods. portlandoregon.gov/parks

29 Portland could be called "Bridgetown" and with good reason - nine unique bridges span the Willamette River connecting the core of downtown to the east side. The **Fremont Bridge** has the longest span of all bridges in Oregon, the **Steel Bridge** is the only double-decker telescoping lift bridge in the world, and the **Broadway Bridge** is a bascule bridge, perhaps better known as a drawbridge.

30 **Macleay Park**, part of 5,200-acre Forest Park in Northwest Portland, has a long and storied past – a true turn-of-the-century drama! The lush, green area became one of the first gifts of land designated for parks in Portland. Today, visitors of all ages and abilities can explore the Witch's Castle and hike over 80 miles of trails. portlandoregon.gov/parks

31 Shortly before sunset in early to mid-September, thousands of Vaux's Swifts roost in the 1925 brick chimney at Chapman Elementary School in Northwest Portland during their annual migration south. **Swift Viewing** has become an annual tradition since the Swifts found the chimney in the 1980s. audubonportland.org/local-birding

SAUVIE ISLAND

PAUL BUNYAN STATUE

PENINSULA PARK

PIP'S ORIGINAL

GRANT PARK

BURNSIDE SKATEPARK

SUNDAY PARKWAYS

LADD'S ADDITION

MAX LIGHT RAIL

MOUNT HOOD

TRILLIUM TRAIL

PORTLAND AERIAL TRAM

TILIKUM CROSSING

4T — COUNCIL CREST PARK

OREGON ZOO

DRAGON BOATS

VOODOO DOUGHNUT

LAN SU CHINESE GARDEN

TANNER SPRINGS PARK

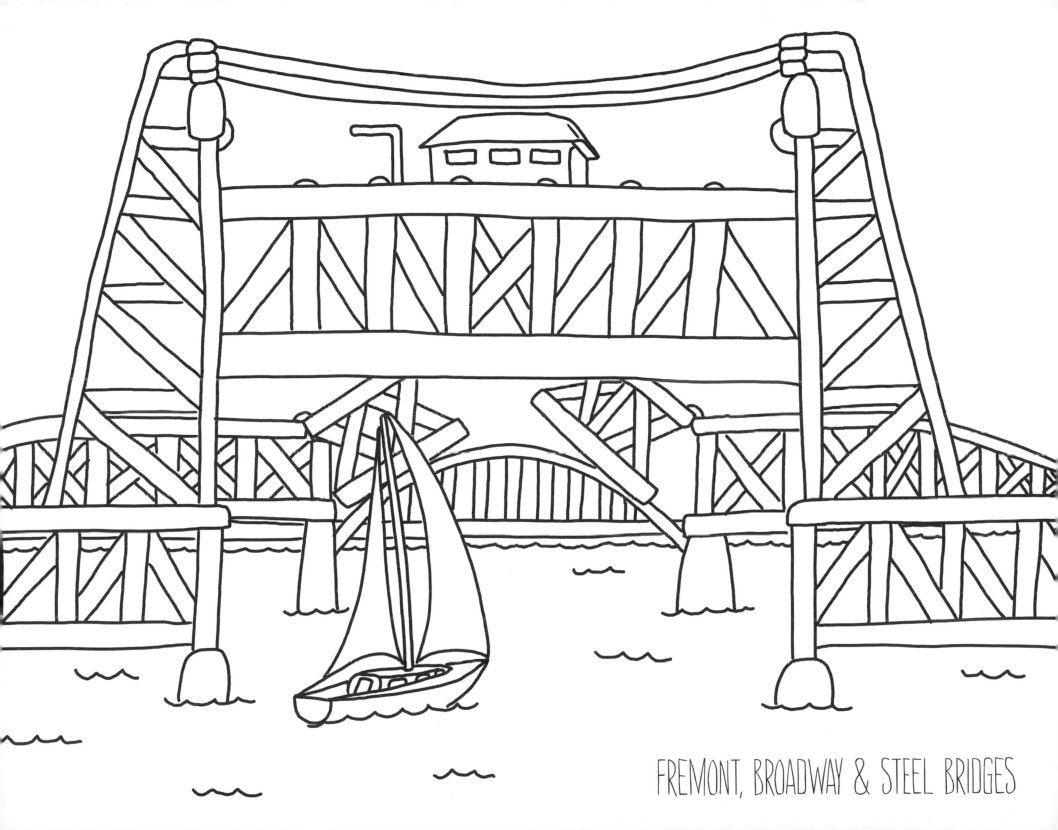

FREMONT, BROADWAY & STEEL BRIDGES

MACLEAY PARK

WILDWOOD TRAIL

DRAW A COLORFUL PLACE IN THE WORLD YOU WOULD LIKE TO EXPLORE

For more cities in this book series please visit: www.colorfulcities.com

100% designed, illustrated and printed in the USA.

Concept, design & text: Laura Lahm
Illustrations: Trevor Essmeier
Map illustration: Steph Calvert
Cover coloring: Julie Knutson

ISBN: 978-0-9898972-2-8

A hearty cappuccino cheers!! to my amazing reviewers, readers, editors and Portland explorers:
Kirk, Astrid, Seth, Jenna, Erika, Emma, Tiffany, Lisa, Lucie, Margot, Maya and Maria.